WALK BESIDE ME
The Joys of Friendship

WALK BESIDE ME

The Joys of Friendship

Yellow Springs, Ohio 45387
ISBN 0-89954-510-6

Contents

Finding a Friend 6

I Want a Friend - The Arrow and the Song - A Mile with Me - Quotations

The Blessing of Friendship 12

The Things I Prize - Count Your Garden - Friendship Is Sweet - Friendship Is Like... - Through Friendship - The Thought of a Friend - A Blessed Thing to Have a Friend - The Glory of Friendship - Quotations

Sharing with a Friend 30

Quotations on the Joy of Giving and Receiving

Being a Friend 34

To a Friend - I Said a Prayer for You Today - Quotations

The Gift of Understanding 40

An Exchange of Thoughts and Feeling - Quotations

The Comfort of Friendship 43

A Breath of Kindness - All Losses Are Restored - If I Can Stop One Heart from Breaking - A Friend in Need - Quotations

The Faithfulness of a Friend 48

Quotations on the Value and Devotion of a Loyal Friend

Old Friends 50

New Friends and Old Friends - The Memory of the Heart - Quotations

God's Friendship 54

Letter from a Friend - Footprints - Quotations

FINDING A FRIEND

I WANT A FRIEND

I want a warm and faithful friend,
To cheer the adverse hour;
Who ne'er to flatter will descend
Nor bend the knee to power;
A friend to chide me when I'm wrong,
My inmost soul to see;
And that my friendship prove as strong
To him as his to me.

—John Quincy Adams

We cannot tell the precise moment when friendship is formed. As in filling a vessel drop by drop, there is at last a drop which makes it run over; so in a series of kindnesses there is at last one which makes the heart run over.

—*James Boswell*

It is chance that makes brothers but hearts that make friends.

—*Von Geibel*

My friends have come to me unsought.
The great God gave them to me.

—*Ralph Waldo Emerson*

The making of friends, who are real friends, is the best token we have of a man's success in life.

—*Edward Everett Hale*

Blessed are they who have the gift of making friends, for it is one of God's best gifts. It involves many things, but above all, the power of going out of one's self, and appreciating whatever is noble and loving in another.

—Thomas Hughes

God evidently does not intend us all to be rich, or powerful, or great, but He does intend us all to be friends.

—Ralph Waldo Emerson

The best that we find in our travels is an honest friend. He is a fortunate voyager who finds many.

—Robert Louis Stevenson

The only way to have a friend is to be one.

—Ralph Waldo Emerson

THE ARROW AND THE SONG

I shot an arrow into the air,
It fell to earth, I knew not where;
For, so swiftly it flew, the sight
Could not follow it in its flight.

I breathed a song into the air,
It fell to earth, I knew not where;
For who has sight so keen and strong,
That it can follow the flight of song?

Long, long afterward, in an oak
I found the arrow, still unbroke;
And the song, from beginning to end,
I found again in the heart of a friend.

—Henry Wadsworth Longfellow

A MILE WITH ME

O who will walk a mile with me
Along life's merry way?
A comrade blithe and full of glee,
Who dares to laugh out loud and free,
And let his frolic fancy play,
Like a happy child, through flowers gay
That fill the field and fringe the way
Where he walks a mile with me.

And who will walk a mile with me
Along life's weary way?
A friend whose heart has eyes to see
The stars shine out o'er the darkening lea,
And the quiet rest at the end o' the day—
A friend who knows, and dares to say,
The brave, sweet words that cheer the way
Where he walks a mile with me.

With such a comrade, such a friend,
I fain would walk till journey's end,
Through summer sunshine, winter rain,
And then?—Farewell, we shall meet
again!

—Henry van Dyke

A true friend is the gift of God, and He only who made hearts can untie them.

—Robert South

Love, and you shall be loved.

—Ralph Waldo Emerson

A friend is a present you give yourself.

—Robert Louis Stevenson

Love is but the discovery of ourselves in others, and the delight in the recognition.

—Alexander Smith

THE BLESSING OF FRIENDSHIP

THE THINGS I PRIZE

These are the things I prize
And hold of dearest worth:
Light of the sapphire skies,
Peace of the silent hills,
Shelter of the forests, comfort of the grass,
Music of birds, murmur of little rills,
Shadows of cloud that swiftly pass,
And, after showers,
The smell of flowers
And of the good brown earth—
And best of all, along the way,
  friendship and mirth.

—Henry van Dyke

The better part of one's life consists of his friendships.

—Abraham Lincoln

And, of all the best things upon earth, I hold that a faithful friend is the best.

—Edward Bulwer-Lytton

It is a good thing to be rich, and a good thing to be strong, but it is a better thing to be loved of many friends.

—Euripides

What wealth it is to have such friends that we cannot think of them without elevation.

—Henry David Thoreau

Of all happinesses, the most charming is that of a firm and gentle friendship. It sweetens all our cares, dispels our sorrows, and counsels us in all extremities.

—Seneca

I count myself in nothing else so happy
As in a soul remembering my good
friends.

—William Shakespeare

The greatest happiness of life is the conviction that we are loved, loved for ourselves, or rather loved in spite of ourselves.

—Victor Hugo

You know my supreme happiness at having one on earth whom I can call a friend.

—Charles Lamb

What joy is better than the news of friends?

—Robert Browning

Few delights can equal the mere presence of one whom we trust utterly.

—George Macdonald

Friendship is a word the very sight of which in print makes the heart warm.

—Augustine Birrell

I awoke this morning with devout thanksgiving for my friends, the old and the new.

—Ralph Waldo Emerson

COUNT YOUR GARDEN

Count your garden by the flowers,
Never by the leaves that fall;
Count your days by golden hours;
Don't remember clouds at all.
Count your nights by stars, not shadows;
Count your years with smiles, not tears;
Count your blessings, not your troubles;
Count your age by friends, not years.

—Author Unknown

A true friend is the greatest of all blessings...

—La Rochefoucauld

Other blessings may be taken away, but if we have acquired a good friend by goodness, we have a blessing which improves in value when others fail.

—W. E. Channing

Life hath no blessing like a prudent friend.

—Euripides

Of all the heavenly gifts
That mortal men commend,
What trusty treasure in the world
Can countervail a friend?

—Nicholas Grimald

FRIENDSHIP IS SWEET

It is a sweet thing, friendship, a dear balm,
A happy and auspicious bird of calm,
Which rides o'er life's ever tumultuous
  Ocean;
A God that broods o'er chaos in
  commotion;
A flower which fresh as Lapland roses are,
Lifts its bold head into the world's
  frore air,
And blooms most radiantly when
  others die,
Health, hope, and youth, and brief
  prosperity;
And with the light and odour of its bloom,
Shining within the dungeon and the tomb;
Whose coming is as light and music are
'Mid dissonance and gloom—a star
Which moves not 'mid the moving
  heavens alone—
A smile among dark frowns—a gentle
  tone
Among rude voices, a beloved light,
A solitude, a refuge, a delight.

—Percy Bysshe Shelley

Every one must have felt that a cheerful friend is like a sunny day, which sheds its brightness on all around...

—Lord Avebury

They seem to take the sun out of the world that take friendship out of life.

—Cicero

My friend peers in on me with merry
Wise face, and though the sky stay dim,
The very light of day, the very
Sun's self comes in with him.

—Algernon Swinburne

FRIENDSHIP IS LIKE...

Friendship—
Like music heard on the waters,
Like pines when the wind passeth by,
Like pearls in the depths of the ocean,
Like stars that enamel the sky,
Like June and the odor of roses,
Like dew and the freshness of morn,
Like sunshine that kisseth the clover,
Like tassels of silk on the corn,
Like mountains that arch the blue heavens,
Like clouds when the sun dippeth low,
Like songs of birds in the forest,
Like brooks where the sweet waters flow,
Like dreams of Arcadian pleasures,
Like colors that gratefully blend,
Like everything breathing of kindness—
Like these is the love of a friend.

—A. P. Stanley

Fame is the scentless sunflower,
with gaudy crown of gold;
But friendship is the breathing rose
with sweets in every fold.
—Oliver Wendell Holmes

The only rose without thorns is friendship.
—Magdeleine de Scudéry

THROUGH FRIENDSHIP

My careful heart was free again,
O friend, my bosom said,
Through thee alone the sky is arched,
Through thee the rose is red;
All things through thee take nobler form,
And look beyond the earth,
The mill-round of our fate appears
A sun-path in thy worth.
Me too thy nobleness has taught
To master my despair;
The fountains of my hidden life
Are through thy friendship fair.

—Ralph Waldo Emerson

Friend is a word of royal tone;
Friend is a poem all alone.

—Persian Poet

A friend may well be reckoned the masterpiece of Nature.

—Ralph Waldo Emerson

Friendship is a single soul dwelling in two bodies.

—Aristotle

Friendship is the highest degree of perfection in society.

—Michel de Montaigne

There is in friendship something of all relations, and something above them all. It is the golden thread that ties the heart of all the world.

—John Evelyn

Friendship is the greatest luxury of life.

—Edward Everett Hale

What a thing friendship is—
World without end!

—Robert Browning

Life is nothing without friendship.

—Cicero

THE THOUGHT OF A FRIEND

Life is to be fortified by many friendships. To love, and to be loved, is the greatest happiness. If I lived under the burning sun of the equator, it would be pleasure for me to think that there were many human beings on the other side of the world who regarded and respected me; I could not live if I were alone upon the earth, and cut off from the remembrance of my fellow-creatures. It is not that a man has occasion often to fall back upon the kindness of his friends; perhaps he may never experience the necessity of doing so; but we are governed by our imaginations, and they stand there as a solid and impregnable bulwark against all the evils of life.

—Sydney Smith

Because of a friend, life is a little stronger, fuller, more gracious thing for the friend's existence, whether he be near or far.

—Arthur C. Benson

True happiness consists not in the multitude of friends, but in their worth and choice.

—Ben Jonson

Perhaps the most delightful friendships are those in which there is much agreement, much disputation, and yet more personal liking.

—George Eliot

Four things are specially the property of friendship: love and affection, security and joy.

—St. Aelred of Rievaulx

A BLESSED THING TO HAVE A FRIEND

A blessed thing it is for any man or woman to have a friend; one human soul whom we can trust utterly; who knows the best and the worst of us, and who loves us in spite of all our faults; who will speak the honest truth to us, while the world flatters us to our face, and laughs at us behind our back; who will give us counsel and reproof in the day of prosperity and self-conceit; but who, again, will comfort and encourage us in the day of difficulty and sorrow, when the world leaves us alone to fight our own battle as we can.

—*Charles Kingsley*

THE GLORY OF FRIENDSHIP

The glory of friendship is not the outstretched hand, nor the kindly smile, nor the joy of companionship; it is the spiritual inspiration that comes to one when he discovers that someone believes in him and is willing to trust him with his friendship.

—Ralph Waldo Emerson

Happy is the house that shelters a friend!

—Ralph Waldo Emerson

Every house where love abides,
And friendship is a guest,
Is surely home, and home-sweet-home:
For there the heart can rest.

—Henry van Dyke

Something like home that is not home is to be desired; it is found in the house of a friend.

—Sir William Temple

The ornament of a house is the friends that frequent it.

—Ralph Waldo Emerson

Sharing With a Friend

Happiness seems made to be shared.
—Pierre Corneille

All who joy would win
Must share it—happiness was born a twin.
—Lord Byron

Not what we give, but what we share,
For the gift without the giver is bare.
—James Russell Lowell

Friendship renders prosperity more brilliant, while it lightens adversity by sharing it and making its burden common.
—Cicero

Friendships multiply joys and divide griefs.

—H. G. Bohn

For there is no man that imparts his joys to his friend, but that he rejoices the more; and no man that imparts his griefs to his friend, but that he grieves the less.

—Francis Bacon

Friendship improves happiness, and abates misery, by doubling our joy, and dividing our grief.

—Joseph Addison

[Friends] cherish each other's hopes. They are kind to each other's dreams.

—Henry David Thoreau

Honest men esteem and value nothing so much in this world as a real friend. Such a one is, as it were, another self, to whom we impart our most secret thoughts, who partakes of our joy, and comforts us in our affliction; add to this, that his company is an everlasting pleasure to us.

—Pilpay

No medicine is more valuable, none more efficacious, none better suited to the cure of all our temporal ills than a friend, to whom we may turn in time of trouble, and with whom we may share our happiness in time of joy.

—St. Aelred of Rievaulx

If, instead of a gem or even a flower, we would cast the gift of a lovely thought into the heart of a friend, that would be giving as the angels give.

—George Macdonald

Love gives itself; it is not bought.

—Henry Wadsworth Longfellow

The love we give away is the only love we keep.

—Elbert Hubbard

Friendship consists of forgetting what one gives and remembering what one receives.

—Alexander Dumas

BEING A FRIEND

It is noble to have a friend, but still nobler to be a friend.

—Richard Wagner

The most I can do for my friend is simply to be his friend.

—Henry David Thoreau

It is not enough to love those who are near and dear to us. We must show them that we do so.

—Lord Avebury

The reward of friendship is itself. The man who hopes for anything else does not understand what true friendship is.

—St. Aelred of Rievaulx

TO A FRIEND

I'd like to be the kind of friend
That you have been to me;
I'd like to be the special help
That you've been glad to be.

I know I'm blessed for only God
Can make a friend like you;
You know just how to cheer me up
Whenever I feel blue.

Could I but have one wish fulfilled,
This one only would it be—
I'd like to be the kind of friend
You've always been to me.

—Author Unknown

The greatest good you can do for another is not just to share your riches, but to reveal to him his own.

—Benjamin Disraeli

Little friends may prove great friends.

—Aesop

A true friend unbosoms freely, advises justly, assists readily, adventures boldly, takes all patiently, defends courageously, and continues a friend unchangeably.

—William Penn

So long as we love, we serve. So long as we are loved by others I would almost say we are indispensable; and no man is useless while he has a friend.

—Robert Louis Stevenson

Friendship...is a miracle which requires constant proofs. It is an exercise of the purest imagination and of the rarest faith.

—Henry David Thoreau

A true friend is somebody who can make us do what we can.

—Ralph Waldo Emerson

Under the magnetism of friendship the modest man becomes bold; the shy, confident; the lazy, active; or the impetuous, prudent and peaceful.

—William Makepeace Thackeray

A friend is one who incessantly pays us the compliment of expecting from us all the virtues, and who can appreciate them in us.

—Henry David Thoreau

I SAID A PRAYER FOR YOU TODAY

I said a prayer for you today
And know God must have heard;
I felt the answer in my heart
Although He spoke not a word.

I didn't ask for wealth or fame
(I knew you wouldn't mind);
I asked for priceless treasures rare
Of a more lasting kind.

I prayed that He'd be near to you
At the start of each new day,
To grant you health and blessings fair,
And friends to share your way.

I asked for happiness for you
In all things great and small,
But that you'd know His loving care
I prayed the most of all.

—Author Unknown

Perfume and incense bring joy to the heart,
and the pleasantness of one's friend
springs from his earnest counsel.

Proverbs 27:9 (NIV)

Two are better than one, because they have a good return for their work: If one falls down, his friend can help him up. But pity the man who falls and has no one to help him up! Also, if two lie down together, they will keep warm. But how can one keep warm alone? Though one may be overpowered, two can defend themselves. A cord of three strands is not quickly broken.

Ecclesiastes 4:9-12 (NIV)

The Gift of Understanding

One of the most beautiful qualities of true friendship is to understand and to be understood.

—*Seneca*

In friendship we find nothing false or insincere; everything is straightforward, and springs from the heart.

—*Cicero*

A friend is a person with whom I may be sincere. Before him, I may think aloud.

—*Ralph Waldo Emerson*

My friend is that one whom I can associate with my choicest thought.

—*Henry David Thoreau*

AN EXCHANGE OF THOUGHTS AND FEELING

The very best thing is good talk, and the thing that helps it most, is friendship. How it dissolves the barriers that divide us, and loosens all constraints, and diffuses itself like some fine old cordial through all the veins of life—this feeling that we understand and trust each other, and wish each other heartily well! Everything into which it really comes is good. It transforms letter-writing from a task to a pleasure. It makes music a thousand times more sweet. The people who play and sing not *at us*, but *to us*, how delightful it is to listen to them! Yes, there is a talkability that can express itself even without words. There is an exchange of thoughts and feeling which is happily alike in speech and in silence. It is quietness pervaded with friendship.

—Henry van Dyke

The language of friendship is not words, but meanings. It is an intelligence above language.

—Henry David Thoreau

The world is so empty if one thinks only of mountains, rivers, and cities; but to know someone who thinks and feels with us, and who, though distant, is close to us in spirit, this makes the earth for us an inhabited garden.

—Johann Wolfgang von Goethe

We do not wish for friends to feed and clothe our bodies...but to do the like office for our spirits.

—Henry David Thoreau

A friend is, as it were, a second self.

—Cicero

THE COMFORT OF FRIENDSHIP

A BREATH OF KINDNESS

Oh, the comfort, the inexpressible comfort of feeling safe with a person, having neither to weigh thoughts nor measure words, but pouring them all right out, just as they are, chaff and grain together; certain that a faithful hand will take and sift them, keep what is worth keeping, and then with the breath of kindness blow the rest away.

—Dinah Maria Craik

ALL LOSSES ARE RESTORED

When to the sessions of sweet silent
thought
I summon up remembrance of things past,
I sigh the lack of many a thing I sought,
And with old woes new wail my dear
time's waste:
Then can I drown an eye, unused to flow,
For precious friends hid in death's dateless
night,
And weep afresh love's long since
cancell'd woe,
And moan the expense of many a vanish'd
sight:
Then can I grieve at grievances foregone,
And heavily from woe to woe tell o'er
The sad account of fore-bemoaned moan,
Which I new pay as if not paid before.
But if the while I think on thee, dear
friend,
All losses are restored and sorrows end.

—William Shakespeare

Friendship is a sheltering tree...

—*Samuel Taylor Coleridge*

The comfort of having a friend may be taken away, but not that of having had one.

—*Seneca*

A friend hath the skill and observation of the best physician; the diligence and vigilance of the best nurse; and the tenderness and patience of the best mother.

—*Lord Clarendon*

Friendship is immeasurably better than kindness.

—*Cicero*

IF I CAN STOP ONE HEART FROM BREAKING

If I can stop one heart from breaking,
I shall not live in vain;
If I can ease one life the aching,
Or cool one pain,
Or help one fainting robin
Unto his nest again,
I shall not live in vain.

— *Emily Dickinson*

A FRIEND IN NEED

"A friend in need," my neighbor said to
me—
"A friend indeed is what I mean to be;
In time of trouble I will come to you
And in the hour of need you'll find me
true."

I thought a bit, and took him by the hand;
"My friend," said I, "you do not
understand
The inner meaning of that simple rhyme—
A friend is what the heart needs all the
time."

—Henry van Dyke

THE FAITHFULNESS OF A FRIEND

A faithful friend is a strong defense: and he that found him, hath found a treasure. Nothing can be compared to a faithful friend, and no weight of gold and silver is able to countervail the goodness of his fidelity.

—The Apocrypha

Love is like the wild rose-briar;
Friendship like the holly-tree.
The holly is dark when the rose-briar
  blooms,
But which will bloom most constantly?

—Emily Bronte

Friendship above all ties does bind the
  heart,
And faith in friendship is the noblest part.

—Lord Orrery

Friendship that follows from the heart cannot be frozen by adversity, as the water that flows from the spring cannot congeal in winter.

—James Fenimore Cooper

True friends visit us in prosperity only when invited, but in adversity, they come without invitation.

—Theophrastus

No distance of place or lapse of time can lessen the friendship of those who are thoroughly persuaded of each other's worth.

—Robert Southey

A friend loves at all times...

Proverbs 17:17 (NIV)

OLD FRIENDS

NEW FRIENDS AND OLD FRIENDS

Make new friends, but keep the old;
Those are silver, these are gold.
New-made friendships, like new wine,
Age will mellow and refine.
Friendships that have stood the test—
Time and change—are surely best;
Brow may wrinkle, hair grow gray;
Friendship never knows decay.
For 'mid old friends, tried and true,
Once more we our youth renew.
But old friends, alas! may die;
New friends must their place supply.
Cherish friendships in your breast—
New is good, but old is best;
Make new friends, but keep the old;
Those are silver, these are gold.

—Joseph Parry

There is no friend like the old friend
Who has shared our morning days,
No greeting like his welcome,
No homage like his praise.

—Oliver Wendell Holmes

Ah, how good it feels—
The hand of an old friend.

—Henry Wadsworth Longfellow

Each year to ancient friendships adds
a ring
As to an oak.

—James Russell Lowell

As gold more splendid from the fire
appears,
Thus friendship brightens by the length
of years.

—Thomas Carlyle

THE MEMORY OF THE HEART

If stores of dry and learned lore we gain,
We keep them in the memory of the brain;
Names, things, and facts—whate'er we
knowledge call—
There is the common ledger for them all;
And images on this cold surface traced
Make slight impression, and are soon
effaced.
But we've a page, more glowing and more
bright,
On which our friendship and our love
to write;
That these may never from the soul depart,
We trust them to the memory of the heart.
There is no dimming, no effacement there;
Each new pulsation keeps the record clear;
Warm, golden letters all the tablet fill,
Nor lose their lustre till the heart stands
still.

—Daniel Webster

Old friends are the great blessing of one's latter years. Half a word conveys one's meaning. They have a memory of the same events, and have the same mode of thinking.

—Horace Walpole

Those friends thou hast,
and their adoption tried,
Grapple them to thy soul
with hoops of steel...

—William Shakespeare

The best mirror is an old friend.

—George Herbert

Old friends are best. King James used to call for his old shoes; they were easiest for his feet.

—John Selden

GOD'S FRIENDSHIP

LETTER FROM A FRIEND

I am writing to say how much I care for you and to say how much I want you to know Me better.

When you awoke this morning I exploded a brilliant sunrise through your window, hoping to get your attention, but you rushed off without even noticing.

Later I noticed you were walking with some friends, so I bathed you in warm sunshine and perfumed the air with nature's sweet scent, and still you didn't notice Me. As you passed by, I shouted to you in a thunderstorm and painted a beautiful rainbow in the sky and you didn't even look.

In the evening, I spilled moonlight onto your face and sent a cool breeze to rest you. As you slept, I watched over you and shared your thoughts, but you were unaware that I was so near.

I have chosen you and hope you will talk to Me soon. Until then I will remain near. I am your friend and love you very much.

Your friend,

Jesus

Wouldst have a friend,
Wouldst know what friend is best?
Have God thy friend,
Who passeth all the rest.

—Thomas Tusser

Jesus only is to be beloved for Himself, for He only is proved good and faithful before all other friends.

—Thomas à Kempis

"...I have called you friends, for everything that I learned from My Father I have made known to you."

John 15:15 (NIV)

Love Him, and keep Him for thy friend, who, when all go away, will not forsake thee, nor suffer thee to perish at the last.

—Thomas à Kempis

FOOTPRINTS

One night a man had a dream. He dreamed he was walking along the beach with the Lord. Across the sky flashed scenes from his life. For each scene, he noticed two sets of footprints in the sand: one belonging to him, and the other to the Lord.

When the last scene of his life flashed before him, he looked back at the footprints in the sand. He noticed that many times along the path of his life there was only one set of footprints. He also noticed that it happened at the very lowest and saddest times in his life. This really bothered him and he questioned the Lord about it.

"Lord, You said that once I decided to follow You, You'd walk with me all the way. But I have noticed that during the most troublesome times in my life, there is only one set of footprints. I don't understand why when I needed You most You would leave me."

The Lord replied, "My son, My precious child, I love you and would never leave you. During your times of trial and suffering, when you see only one set of footprints, it was then that I carried you."

—Author Unknown

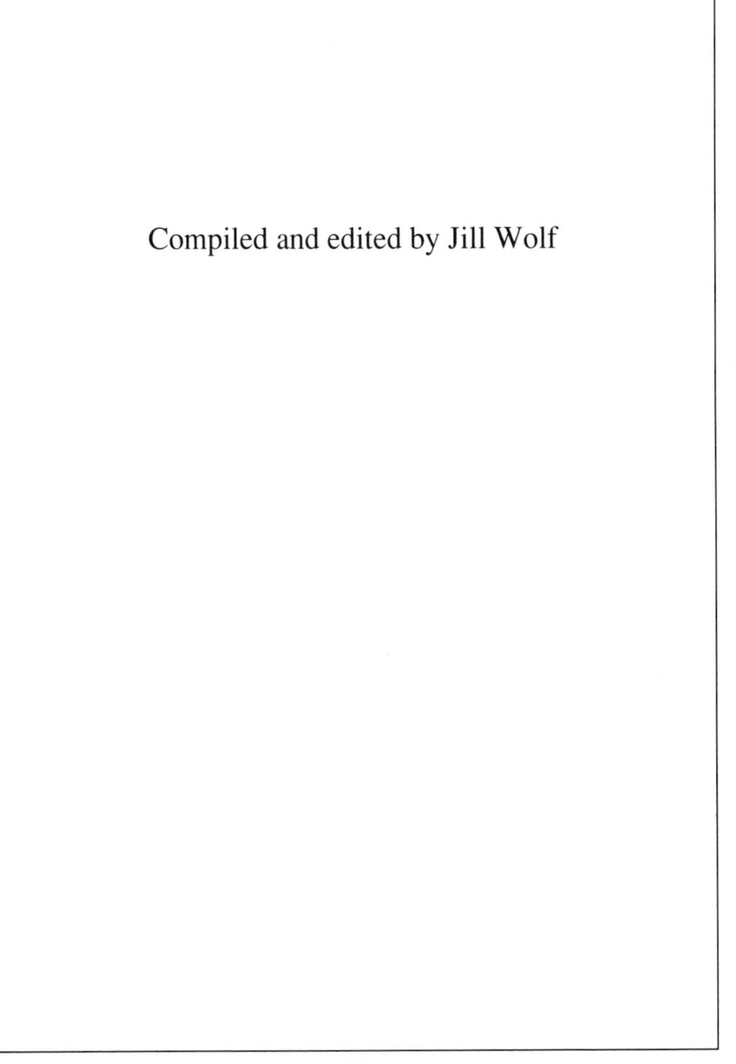

Compiled and edited by Jill Wolf